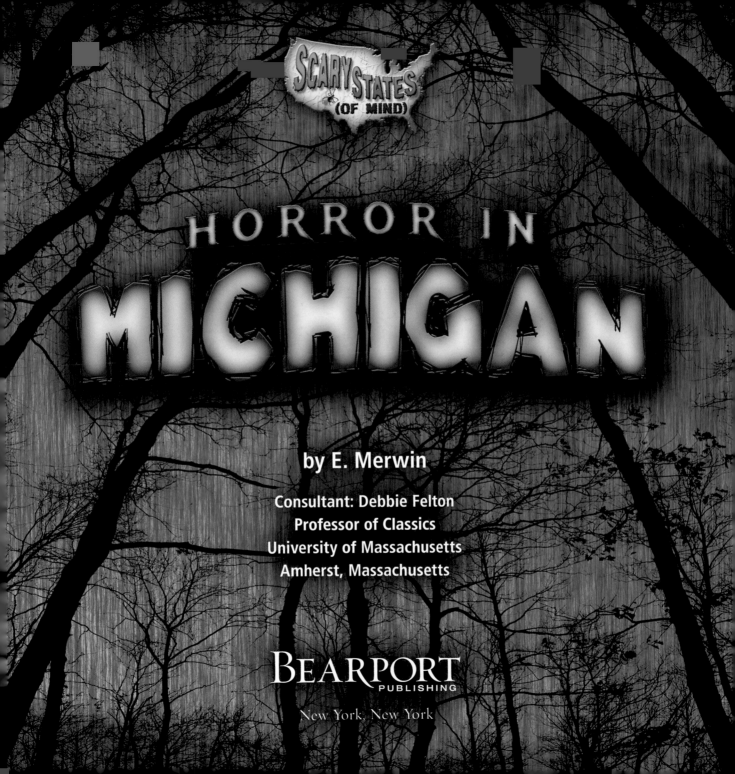

SCARY STATES (OF MIND)

HORROR IN MICHIGAN

by E. Merwin

Consultant: Debbie Felton
Professor of Classics
University of Massachusetts
Amherst, Massachusetts

BEARPORT PUBLISHING

New York, New York

Credits

Cover, © Thomas Barrat/Shutterstock, © Sergiy1975/Shutterstock, and © ehrlif/Shutterstock; TOC, © ehrlif/Shutterstock; 4–5, © bramgino/Shutterstock, © Jane Rix/Shutterstock, © chrisdorney/Shutterstock, © Jenn Huls/Shutterstock, and © Eric Isselee/Shutterstock; 6, © Dark Shadows/CC BY-SA 4.0; 7, © James Schaedig/Alamy; 8–9, © Google Maps Data 2018, © Boonchuay1970/Shutterstock, and © Jogendra Kumar/Shutterstock; 10, © Ying Onwan/Shutterstock; 11, © Dimitry Bobroff/Alamy; 12, © merzzie/Shutterstock and © lawcain/iStock; 13, © Tymonko Galyna/Shutterstock and © Sorapop Udomsri/Shutterstock; 14T, Public Domain; 14B, © Attapol Yiemsiriwut/Shutterstock; 15, © Doug Lemke/Shutterstock; 16, © Ravinee wanmadh/Shutterstock; 17, © Selector Jonathan Photography; 18, © Kamira/Shutterstock; 19, © Brandon Bartoszek; 20, © Doug Copeland; 21L, © Brandon Bartoszek; 21R, Public Domain; 23, © Darryl Brooks/Shutterstock; 24, © Fotokita/Shutterstock.

Publisher: Kenn Goin
Senior Editor: Joyce Tavolacci
Creative Director: Spencer Brinker
Photo Researcher: Thomas Persano
Cover: Kim Jones

Library of Congress Cataloging-in-Publication Data

Names: Merwin, E., author.
Title: Horror in Michigan / by E. Merwin.
Description: New York : Bearport Publishing Company, Inc., 2020. | Series: Scary states (of mind) | Includes bibliographical references and index.
Identifiers: LCCN 2019009585 (print) | LCCN 2019017817 (ebook) | ISBN 9781642805741 (Ebook) | ISBN 9781642805208 (library)
Subjects: LCSH: Haunted places—Michigan—Juvenile literature. | Ghosts—Michigan—Juvenile literature. | Michigan—Miscellanea—Juvenile literature.
Classification: LCC BF1472.U6 (ebook) | LCC BF1472.U6 M4649 2020 (print) | DDC 133.109774—dc23
LC record available at https://lccn.loc.gov/2019009585

For more information, write to Bearport Publishing Company, Inc., 45 West 21st Street, Suite 3B, New York, New York 10010. Printed in the United States of America.

10 9 8 7 6 5 4 3 2 1

CONTENTS

Horror in Michigan

Michigan winters are freezing! But the most chilling thing about this state is its ghostly **residents**. Some dwell in hotels, others in shallow graves. All their stories will leave you ice cold!

Get ready to read four terrifying tales about Michigan. Turn the page . . . if you dare.

Stairway to Hell

Lake Forest Cemetery, Grand Haven

In this Michigan **graveyard,** an old staircase rises out of the ground. It's called the Stairway to Hell. Ghosts are believed to climb its crumbling steps.

Some people say that the **spirits** of the dead must walk to the top of the stairway. If they see a white light, they will find peace. If not, they will go to a darker **realm.**

Lake Forest Cemetery

The Stairway to Hell in Lake Forest Cemetery

Lake Forest Cemetery opened in 1873.

Near the stairway is an area called Potter's Field. It's a place where poor people are buried. There are over 1,400 graves but no gravestones. One day, a **psychic** visited this place. He felt a heavy sadness.

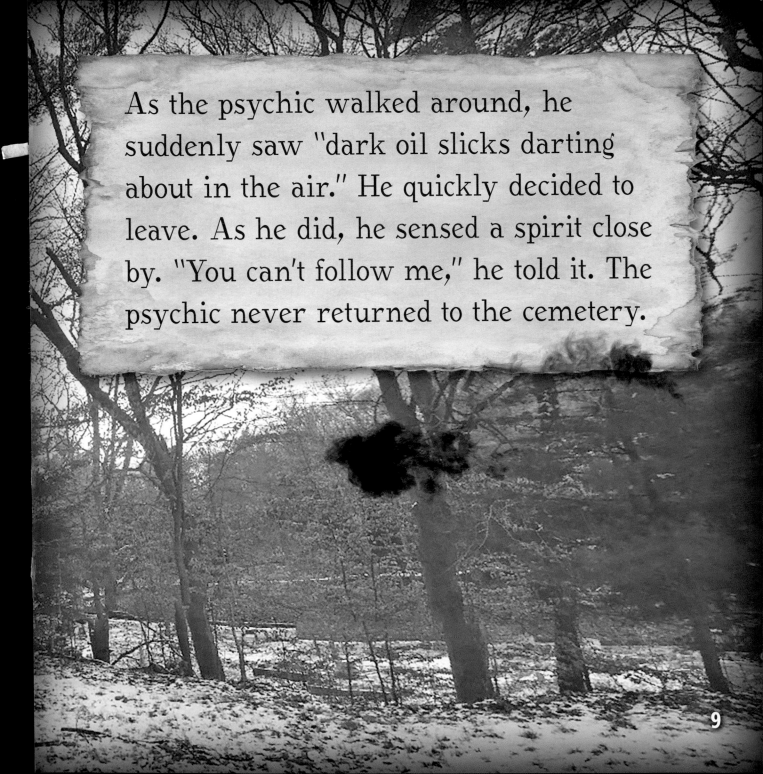

As the psychic walked around, he suddenly saw "dark oil slicks darting about in the air." He quickly decided to leave. As he did, he sensed a spirit close by. "You can't follow me," he told it. The psychic never returned to the cemetery.

SLEEP AT YOUR OWN RISK

Grand Hotel, Mackinac Island

This Michigan hotel is built on an **ancient** graveyard. Over 1,000 years ago, Native Americans buried their chiefs there. Later, soldiers were laid to rest on the same spot.

Construction of the hotel began in 1884. As they dug, workers found many human skeletons. It's no surprise that spirits are said to haunt the building.

Grand Hotel

There were so many skeletons that workers couldn't move all of them. So they built the hotel on top of them!

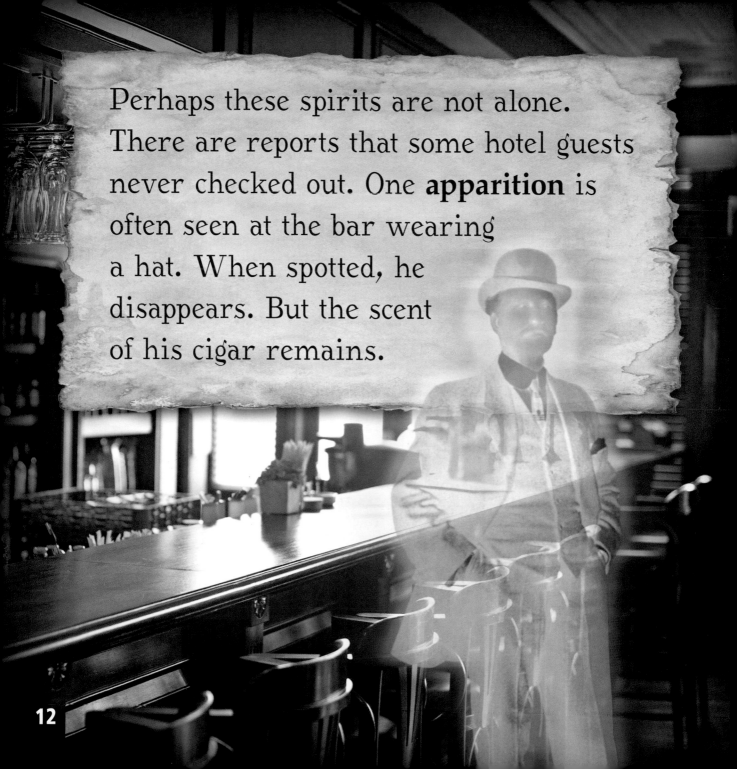

Perhaps these spirits are not alone. There are reports that some hotel guests never checked out. One **apparition** is often seen at the bar wearing a hat. When spotted, he disappears. But the scent of his cigar remains.

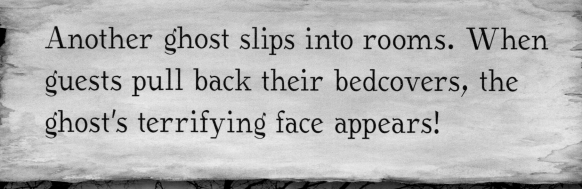

Another ghost slips into rooms. When guests pull back their bedcovers, the ghost's terrifying face appears!

Return of the Keepers

Grand Traverse Lighthouse, Leelanau State Park

In this old Michigan lighthouse, many of its **keepers** have returned from the dead.

Peter Nelson

Peter Nelson was a keeper of the lighthouse from 1874 to 1890. He died of old age in 1892. Visitors often hear the heavy steps of his boots. At the front desk, one worker watched Peter's ghost taking off its boots!

Out of seven brothers, Peter Nelson was the only one who did not die at sea.

Grand Traverse Lighthouse

The spirits of other former keepers have also been seen at the lighthouse. Keeper John Marken and his wife died in 1967 after they crashed their car on Christmas Eve. Some say their ghosts wander the grounds.

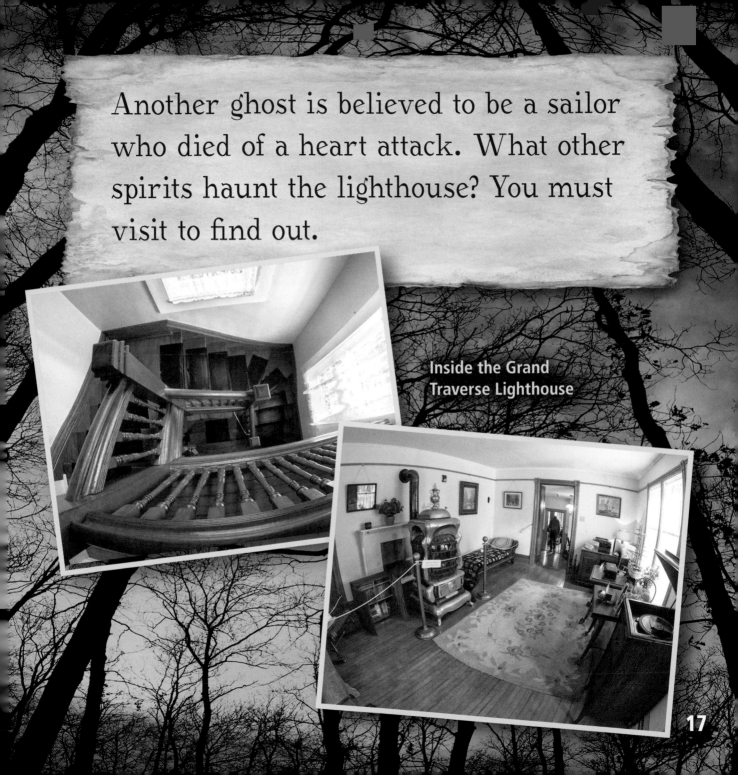

Another ghost is believed to be a sailor who died of a heart attack. What other spirits haunt the lighthouse? You must visit to find out.

Inside the Grand Traverse Lighthouse

17

THE ANGEL OF MUSKEGON

The Hackley Public Library, Muskegon

A stone angel stands over the **tomb** of Charles Hackley. Some say Charles was a real-life angel who helped save his town.

In the 1860s, Muskegon was run down. Charles used his own money to build a library and other buildings. The people of Muskegon were overjoyed. Charles Hackley died in 1905. But, it seems, he never left the library nor the town he loved.

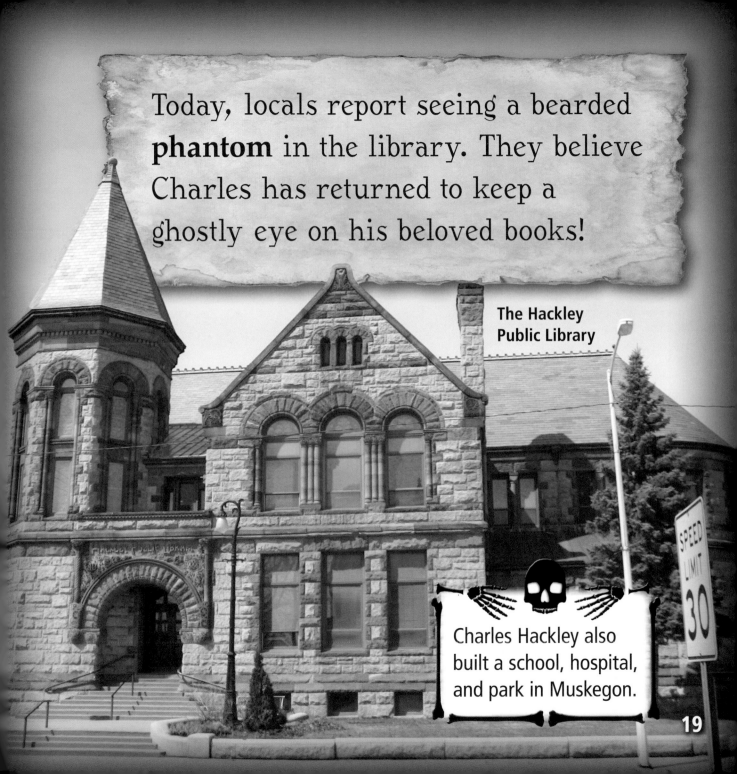

Today, locals report seeing a bearded **phantom** in the library. They believe Charles has returned to keep a ghostly eye on his beloved books!

The Hackley
Public Library

Charles Hackley also built a school, hospital, and park in Muskegon.

SPEED LIMIT 30

The spirit of Charles Hackley has also visited his family's home. One woman saw a see-through man in a bedroom. A week later, the woman found an old photo in the attic. The man in the photo looked just like the ghost she had seen.

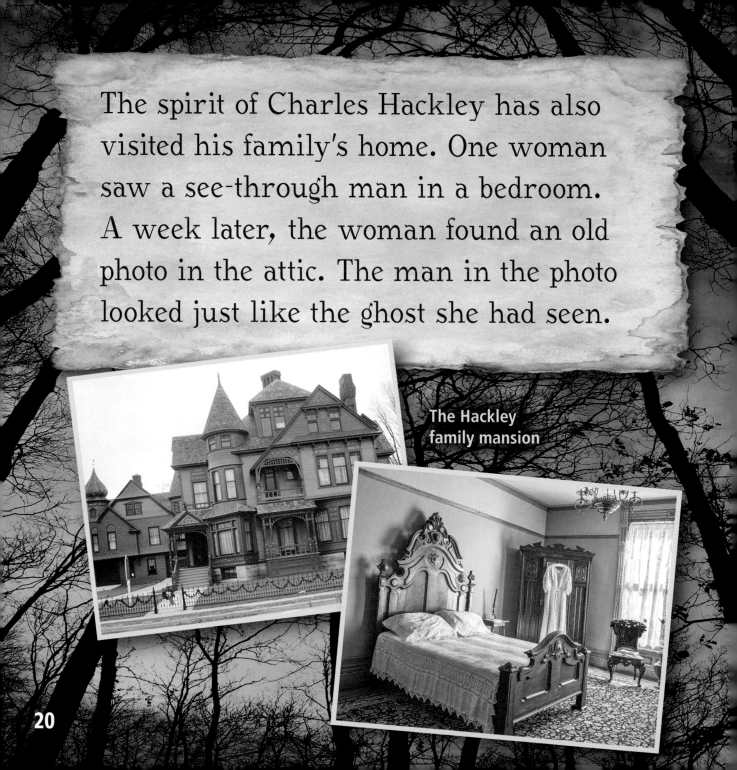

The Hackley family mansion

When she visited the Hackley Library, she saw a **portrait** of Charles Hackley. It was the same man!

Charles Hackley

Spooky Spots in Michigan

Grand Traverse Lighthouse
Visit the lighthouse, but be careful not to disturb the ghosts.

Lake Superior

CANADA

Grand Hotel
Mingle with some phantom guests.

WISCONSIN

Lake Michigan

Lake Huron

The Hackley Public Library
Meet the town's most famous ghost.

MICHIGAN

CANADA

UNITED STATES

MEXICO

Lake Forest Cemetery
Climb a crooked staircase with the spirits of the dead.

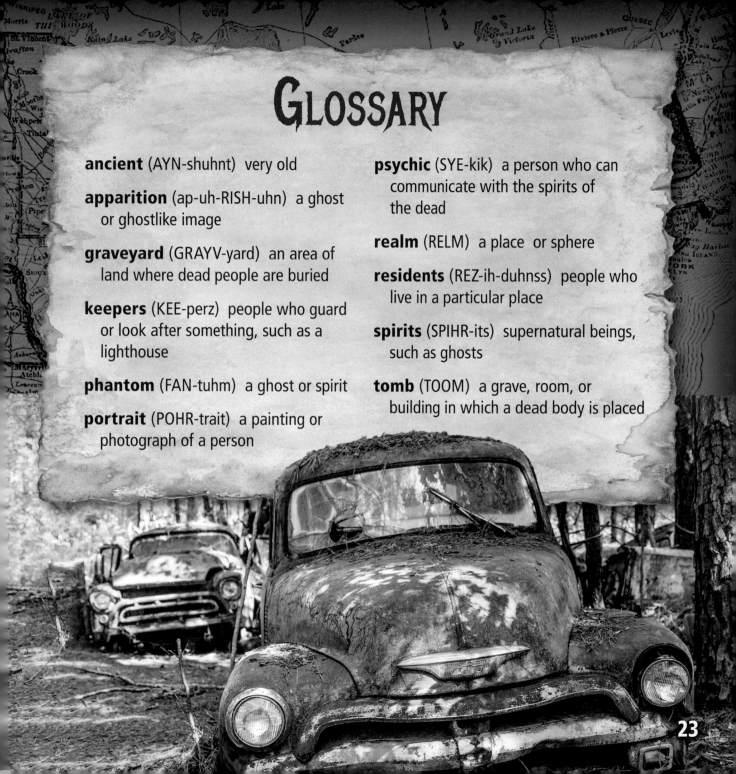

GLOSSARY

ancient (AYN-shuhnt) very old

apparition (ap-uh-RISH-uhn) a ghost or ghostlike image

graveyard (GRAYV-yard) an area of land where dead people are buried

keepers (KEE-perz) people who guard or look after something, such as a lighthouse

phantom (FAN-tuhm) a ghost or spirit

portrait (POHR-trait) a painting or photograph of a person

psychic (SYE-kik) a person who can communicate with the spirits of the dead

realm (RELM) a place or sphere

residents (REZ-ih-duhnss) people who live in a particular place

spirits (SPIHR-its) supernatural beings, such as ghosts

tomb (TOOM) a grave, room, or building in which a dead body is placed

Index

Read More

Markovics, Joyce. *Chilling Cemeteries (Tiptoe Into Scary Places).* New York: Bearport (2017).

Rudolph, Jessica. *Spooky Libraries (Tiptoe Into Scary Places).* New York: Bearport (2017).

Learn More Online

To learn more about the horror in Michigan, visit:

www.bearportpublishing.com/ScaryStates

About the Author

E. Merwin is an author who is fascinated by people—
in this life and beyond!